Knitgrrl
HATS

Knitgrrl Hats

ISBN 13 (print): 978-1-937513-88-7

First edition

Published by http://www.cooperativepress.com

Patterns, charts ©2018 Shannon Okey

Photos ©2018 Shannon Okey except pages 10, 38, 41 (Amber Patrick) and pages 14, 19, 24, 29, 48, 53, 54 (Jenn Kidd)

Models: Shannon Okey, Jenny Barnett Rohrs, Breaya Wilson, Jenn Kidd, Danielle Marx, Alison Taylor, Daniella Cortez, Simone Renee Dugay, Soren Roberts, Jennifer Davis, Kate Snow

Technical Editor: Andi Smith

Book layout: Shannon Okey and Kim Saar with special thanks to Emily Kuhn for cover help.

Every effort has been made to ensure that all the information in this book is accurate at the time of publication; however, Cooperative Press neither endorses nor guarantees the content of external links referenced in this book.

If you have questions or comments about this book, or need information about licensing, custom editions, special sales, or academic/corporate purchases, please contact Cooperative Press: info@cooperativepress.com or 10252 Berea Rd, Cleveland, Ohio 44102 USA

No part of this book may be reproduced in any form, except brief excerpts for the purpose of review, without prior written permission of the publisher. Thank you for respecting our copyright.

Knitgrrl
HATS

Cooperative Press
Cleveland, Ohio

Patterns

Brandywine, 6

Cydonia, 10

Dalal, 14

Darlington, 20

Elling, 24

Forsythe, 30

Koray, 34

Signy, 38

Sini, 44

Wickson, 48

Xantho, 54

Intro

This project was overambitious from the very beginning. I looked at my (considerable) yarn stash and declared a problem with the sheer amount. So naturally, I called my tech editor Andi Smith with a ridiculous idea: why not release a pattern a week for a year, and run a Patreon to help fund it? Yarn we had, but sample knitting is not cheap (nor should it be), and we also knew what other kinds of expenses to expect along the way after working on so many other projects together.

Andi is more than just my friend and tech editor. She is my co-conspirator, collaborator, enabler, right hand, left brain, and heart. We are teaching road trip road warriors, fiber show booth buddies, sounding boards, middle of the night text messagers and more. Without Andi's skills, this project would never have happened. She takes my gigantic, wild ideas and figures out how to make them reality, and she encourages me along the way without actually making me feel as if perhaps I should tone it down a bit. This book is part of the result!

You can find all the single patterns from this project on Ravelry:
- https://www.ravelry.com/patterns/sources/knitgrrl-patreon

I plan to continue the Patreon after the initial 52 pattern releases:
- https://www.patreon.com/knitgrrl

I knit Brandywine, but sample knitters are the unsung heroes of the knit design industry, and don't get nearly enough pay or credit for all their hard work! Here's who helped me bring these designs to life. Many of them are also designers. Look for them on Ravelry!
- Meg Roke: Cydonia, Darlington, Elling, Sini
- Michelle Kroll: Dalal, Koray
- Jen Coican Hovis: Forsythe, Signy
- Sarah Jo Burch: Wickson
- Beth Talisman: Xantho

At the end of the book you'll also find a list of Patreon patrons. Their project support funded sample knitting, photography, tech editing and all the other expenses required to bring this to life. Thank you, everyone!

Brandywine

After this pattern was first released for the #knitgrrl52 project, at the last minute, both Andi Smith (my tech editrix extraordinaire) and I ended up knitting entirely new samples while we were away at Indie Knit and Spin in Pittsburgh. Brandywine is fast, fun and super comfy to wear. Technically, I was thinking of the crinkly-topped heirloom tomatoes because the first sample was red but I don't know what those are called so let's name this after another fave tomato of mine...

Size
S (M, L)

Shown in Size L

Finished Measurements
Circumference: 17.5 (20, 22.5) inches / 44.5 (50.75, 57.15) cm

Height: 8 inches / 20.25 cm

Materials
Malabrigo Worsted (100% Merino; 210 yds / 192m per 100g skein); color: Vermillion; 1 skein

US#8 / 5mm needles, configured for knitting in the round

18 or more REMOVABLE stitch markers

Yarn needle

Gauge
16 sts and 24 rows = 4 inches / 10 cm in stockinette stitch

Pattern

Brim

Cast on 72 (81, 90) sts and join to work in the round, being careful not to twist. Place marker at beginning of round.

Rnds 1–9: *P1, k1; repeat from * to end of rnd.

(Optional short rows begin here: you can skip these and opt to make the ribbing a little deeper, or not—it's your choice.

The short rows create a pointed accent in the edge of the hat that's meant to be worn to one side of your face).

Note - on RS rows, you'll be wrapping the next purl stitch, on WS rows, you'll be wrapping a knit stitch - which is a purl stitch on the RS, thus hiding the wraps within the purl bumps on all the wrapped RS sts.

Rnd 10: Work 26 (30, 34) sts in pattern, W&T.

Row 11: Work 24 (28, 32) sts in pattern, W&T.

Row 12: Work 22 (26, 30) sts in pattern, W&T.

Continue in this manner, working two less sts each row, and wrapping and turning, until you have 2 sts left.

Next rnd. Work one full round, in pattern, without wrapping or turning across all sts. Place a marker to denote new start of rnd.

Body

Rnd 1: Knit, placing markers every 8 (9, 10) sts - 9 sections in all.

Rnd 2: *Knit to 1 st before marker, kfb, sm, kfb; repeat from * to end of rnd. 90 (99, 108) sts.

Rnd 3: Knit.

Repeat Rnds 2 and 3 four times more - 144 (162, 180) sts.

Work without shaping until hat measures 6 inches / 15.25 cm.

Crown

Rnd 1: Knit, moving each marker 8 (9, 10) sts to the left (re-centering them between each set of increases).

Rnd 2: *Ssk, k to 2 sts before next marker, k2tog; repeat from * to end of rnd. 126 (144, 162) sts.

Rnd 3: Knit.

Repeat Rnds 2 and 3 until 14 (16, 18) sts remain.

Next rnd: *K2tog; repeat to end of rnd. 7 (8, 9) sts.

Break yarn, and thread through remaining live sts. Pull tight to secure, and weave in all ends.

Cydonia

Cydonia oblonga is the botanical name for the common quince, an underappreciated fruit that I love (and this is knit from Quince & Co yarn, so...). When cooked, quince becomes a beautiful rosy pink like this hat! If you've never tried it but love cheese, seek out Spanish membrillo paste made from quince...it's great with salty, sharp cheeses and crackers. And if you can find quince locally, it's super easy to make in a slow cooker, too.

Size
Adult S/M (L, XL); shown in size S/M

Finished Measurements
Circumference: 20 (22.25, 24.5) inches / 51 (56.5, 62) cm

Length: 8 (8.5, 9) inches / 20.5 (21.5, 23) cm

Materials
Quince & Co. Lark (100% American wool; 134 yds / 123m per 50g skein); color: Petal; 1 (1, 2) skeins

US#7 / 4.5mm 16-inch circular needles

US#7 dpns

US#6 / 4mm 16-inch circular needles

Stitch markers

Yarn needle

Gauge
18 sts and 25 rnds = 4 inches / 10cm in reverse stockinette stitch on larger needles

Pattern Notes
This hat is worked in the round from the bottom beginning with a single rib rim. The body of the hat features a pyramid rib pattern followed by reverse stockinette stitch crown. The crown is worked in swirl decreases keeping with the reverse stockinette stitch pattern.

Stitches and Techniques

Single Rib

All Rnds: [K1, p1], to end.

Pyramid Rib

Rnds 1–4: [P1, k1] 4 times, p2.

Rnds 5–8: P2, [k1, p1] 3 times, p2.

Rnds 9–12: P3, k1, p1, k1, p4.

Rnds 13–16: P4, k1, p5.

Reverse Stockinette Stitch

All Rnds: Purl.

Pattern

CO 90 (100, 110) sts using smaller needles and long tail cast on or preferred method of cast on.

Pm and join to work in the rnd.

Work in single rib for 12 (12, 16) rnds.

Change to larger needles.

Work Rnds 1–16 of chart, repeating 10-st patt 9 (10, 11) times. Purl 13 (14, 11) rnds.

Beg crown dec - switch to dpns as needed.

Next Rnd for L and XL sizes only: [K - (23, 53), k2tog], to end. 90 (96, 108) sts.

Dec Set-up Rnd: [P13 (14, 16) sts, p2tog, pm], to end. 84 (90, 102) sts.

Dec Rnd: [Purl to last 2 sts before m, p2tog, sm], to end.

Rep last dec rnd until 6 sts rem.

Cut a 6" / 15 cm tail to thread through rem live sts. Pull tight and secure.

Using a tapestry needle, weave in all ends.

Steam or wet block to measurements.

Chart

	10	9	8	7	6	5	4	3	2	1	
	•	•	•	•	•		•	•	•	•	16
	•	•	•	•	•		•	•	•	•	15
	•	•	•	•	•		•	•	•	•	14
	•	•	•	•	•		•	•	•	•	13
	•	•	•	•		•		•	•	•	12
	•	•	•	•		•		•	•	•	11
	•	•	•	•		•		•	•	•	10
	•	•	•	•		•		•	•	•	9
	•	•	•		•		•		•	•	8
	•	•	•		•		•		•	•	7
	•	•	•		•		•		•	•	6
	•	•	•		•		•		•	•	5
	•	•		•		•		•		•	4
	•	•		•		•		•		•	3
	•	•		•		•		•		•	2
	•	•		•		•		•		•	1

☐ Knit

⊡ Purl

Dalal

Dalal is a woman's given name in Arabic that means "to touch with love and kindness"—which sounds a lot like knitting to me! This gorgeous MadTosh yarn does an amazing job of displaying texture, and the yarn color is dreamy.

Size
S (M, L, 1X, 2X)

Finished Measurements
Intended to be worn with approximately 1 inch of negative ease

Height: 6.5 (7, 8.5, 9, 9.5) inches / 16.5 (17.75, 21.5, 22.75, 24) cm

Circumference: 16 (18, 20, 22, 24) inches / 40.5 (45.75, 50.75, 55.75, 61) cm

Materials
Madelinetosh Tosh Vintage (100% Merino; 210 yds / 192m per skein); color: Cousteau; 1 skein

US#7 / 4.5mm needles configured for circular knitting

Stitch marker

Yarn needle

Gauge
20 sts and 24 rounds = 4 inches / 10cm in pattern stitch

Stitches and Techniques
Dalal stitch pattern

Rnd 1: [K1tbl, p1] 4 times.

Rnds 2, 3, 4: as Rnd 1.

Rnd 5: [K1tbl, p1] twice, k1tbl, yo, ssk, p1.

Rnd 6: [K1tbl, p1] twice, [k1, p1] twice.

Rnd 7: K1tbl, p1, k1tbl, k2tog, yo, p1, yo, ssk.

Rnd 8: As Rnd 6.

Rnd 9: Ssk, p1, k2tog, yo, k1, p1, k1, yo.

Rnd 10: [K1, p1] 4 times.

Rnd 11: Yo, sl1, k2tog, psso, yo, p1, [k1, p1] twice.

Rnd 12: K3, p1, [k1, p1] twice. At the end of Rnd 12, arrange the sts as follows: Slip the last st of the rnd to the beginning of the next rnd.

Rnd 13: P1, k1, yo, ssk, p1, wrap 3 st.

Rnd 14: [P1, k1] 4 times.

Rnd 15: K2tog, yo, p1, yo, ssk, k1, p1, k1.

Rnd 16: As Rnd 14.

Rnd 17: Yo, k1tbl, p1, k1tbl, yo, ssk, p1, k2tog.

Rnd 18: [P1, k1tbl] twice, [p1, k1] twice.

Rnd 19: P1, [k1tbl, p1] twice, yo, sl1, k2tog, psso, yo.

Rnd 20: P1, [k1tbl, p1] twice, k3.

Rnds 21–24: [P1, k1tbl] 4 times.

Pattern

Using your favorite stretchy method, cast on 80 (88, 104, 112, 120) sts, and being careful not to twist, join to work in the round, adding a stitch marker to note the beginning of the round.

Work Rnds 1–24 from either the chart or the pattern name stitch pattern words across each rnd.

Continue working in p1, k1tbl rib until hat measures 4.5 (5, 6.5, 7, 7.5) inches / 11.5 (12.75, 16.5, 17.75, 19) cm from cast on.

Work crown decreases as follows:

Rnd 1: *[P1, k1tbl] 3 times, p1, k2tog; repeat from * to end of rnd. 70 (77, 91, 98, 105) sts.

Rnd 2: *[P1, k1tbl] 3 times, k1tbl; repeat from * to end of rnd.

Rnd 3: *[P1, k1tbl] twice, p1, k2tog; repeat from * to end of rnd. 60 (66, 78, 84, 90) sts.

Rnd 4: *P1, k1tbl; repeat from * to end of rnd.

Rnd 5: *[P1, k1tbl] twice, k2tog; repeat from * to end of rnd. 50 (55, 65, 70, 75) sts.

Rnd 6: *[P1, k1tbl] twice, k1tbl; repeat from * to end of rnd.

Rnd 7: *P1, k1tbl, p1, k2tog; repeat from * to end of rnd. 40 (44, 52, 56, 60) sts.

Rnd 8: *P1, k1tbl; repeat from * to end of rnd.

Rnd 9: *P1, k1tbl, k2tog; repeat from * to end of rnd. 30 (33, 39, 42, 45) sts.

Rnd 10: *P1, k1tbl, k1tbl; repeat from * to end of rnd.

Rnd 11: *P1, k2tog; repeat from * to end of rnd. 20 (22, 26, 28, 30) sts.

Rnd 12: *P1, k1tbl; repeat from * to end of rnd.

Rnd 13: *K2tog; repeat from * to end of rnd. 10 (11, 13, 14, 15)

Rnd 14: K0 (1, 1, 0, 1), *k2tog; repeat from * to end of rnd. 5 (6, 7, 7, 8) sts.

Finishing

Break yarn, and thread through live sts. Pull the circle tight, and weave in all ends. Block.

Key

Symbol	Meaning
☐	No stitch
•	Purl
☐	Knit
Ꝗ	K1tbl
○	YO
/	K2tog
\	Ssk
人	Sl1, k2tog, psso
←3→	Wrap 3 st

Dalal Chart

Dalal crown decreases

Darlington

Most textured stitch patterns get lost when knitting with variegated or self-striping yarn. This hat pattern is the exception. It showcases the beautiful transitions of color in the Noro Silk Garden yarn. The Trinity Stitch pattern featured pops and since it is knit at a slightly looser gauge, it almost looks like lace and reduces the look of bulk and the weight of wool.

Size
Adult small (adult medium)

Finished Measurements
Circumference: 19.75 (21) inches / 50 (53.5) cm - intended to be worn with about an inch of negative ease

Length: 7.5 (8.5) inches / 19 (21.5) cm

Materials
Noro Silk Garden Sock (40% wool, 25% silk, 25% nylon, 10% mohair; 328 yds / 300m per 100g skein / (3.53 oz); 1 skein in color 245-S

US#3 / 3.25mm 16-inch circular needles for brim of hat

US#7 / 4.5mm 16-inch circular needles and dpns for body of hat

Stitch markers

Yarn needle

Gauge
22 sts and 30 rnds = 4 inches / 10 cm in single rib stitch on smaller needles, stretched

20 sts and 28 rnds = 4 inches / 10 cm in Trinity stitch on larger needles or size needed to obtain correct gauge

Pattern Notes
This textured hat is worked in the round from the bottom up. The brim is worked in a single rib stitch. The body of the hat is worked in a looser gauge trinity stitch. The crown is worked in concentric circle decreases.

Stitches and Techniques

Single Rib (worked over an even number of sts)

All rnds: [K1, p1] to end.

Trinity Stitch (multiple of 4 sts)

Rnd 1: Purl.

Rnd 2: [P1, k1, p1] into the next st, k3tog

Rnd 3: Purl.

Rnd 4: K3tog, [p1, k1, p1] into the next st

Pattern

Brim

Using US#3 / 3.25mm circular needle, and long tail method, cast on 108 (116) sts, place a marker to denote beginning of rnd, and join to work in the round.

Work the Single Rib for 2.25 (2.5) inches / 5.75 (6.5) cm

Body of Hat

Switch to US#7 / 4.5mm needles.

Work Trinity Stitch repeating 4-st pattern 27 (29) times.

Continue in established pattern until hat measures 5.5 (6) inches / 14 (15.5) cm or 2 (2.5) inches / 5 (6) cm less than desired length, ending after the fourth row of the stitch pattern.

Crown

Begin crown decreases and switch to dpns as needed.

Medium size only:

Next Rnd: [P13, p2tog, p12, p2tog] four times. (108 sts)

Work Rnds 2–4 of Trinity Stitch pattern.

All sizes:

Rnd 1: *P1, p2tog; repeat from * to end. 72 sts.

Rnds 2–4: Work Rnds 2–4 of Trinity Stitch pattern.

Rnd 5: *P1, p2tog; repeat from * to end. 48 sts.

Rnds 6–8: Work Rnds 2–4 of Trinity Stitch pattern.

Rnd 9: *P2tog; repeat from * to end. 24 sts.

Rnds 10–12: Work Rnds 2–4 of Trinity Stitch pattern.

Rnd 13: *P2tog; repeat from * to end. 12 sts.

Rnd 14: *P2tog; repeat from * to end. 6 sts.

Cut a 6 inch / 15cm tail to thread through remaining live sts. Pull tight and secure.

Finishing

Weave in all ends and steam or wet block to measurements.

Elling set

This quick-knit set is named after a bog person find, specifically Elling Woman. Recently I took a metalsmithing class and my artist aunt kept telling me everything I made looked as if it had been found in a bog. This is high praise with the two of us, let me tell you. And since the yarn color IS "Bog of Eternal Stench," well...

Required Skills

Basic knitting skills

Knitting in the round

Decreases

Working simple stitches from chart and written instructions

Hat Sizes

S (M, L, XL); shown in size M

Finished Measurements

Circumference: 18 (20, 21.75 23.5) inches / 45.5 (51, 55, 59.5) cm

Length: 8.5 (9, 9.5, 10) inches / 21.5 (23, 24, 25.5) cm

Sizing note: this hat is intended to be worn slouchy, so aim for a size that either matches your head circumference, or even larger. It's a personal preference for just how slouchy you want it.

Materials

Cephalopod Traveller (100% merino; 280 yds / 256m per 114g skein); color: Bog of Eternal Stench; 1 skein

US#5 / 3.75mm 16-inch circular needle

US#6 / 4mm 16-inch circular needle

US#6 / 4mm needles for small circumference, DPNs, 1 long circular or 2 short circulars as you prefer

or needles needed to obtain gauge

Stitch markers

Yarn needle

Gauge

21 sts and 27 rnds = 4 inches / 10cm in stockinette stitch on larger needles or size needed to obtain correct gauge

Pattern Notes

This slouchy hat is worked in the round from the bottom up beginning with smaller needles and a seeded rib stitch rim. The body of the hat is worked in repeats of the roman stitch pattern in larger needles. The crown is worked in stockinette stitch in swirl decreases.

Stitches and Techniques

Seeded Rib

Rnd 1: *K1,p1; rep from * to end of rnd.

Rnd 2: Knit.

Roman Stitch

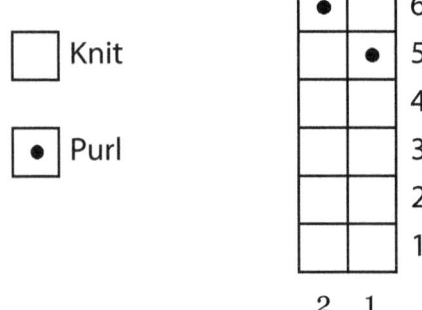

Rnds 1-4: Knit.

Rnd 5: *P1, k1; rep from * to end of rnd.

Rnd 6: *K1, p1; rep from * to end of rnd.

Stockinette Stitch

All Rnds: Knit.

Pattern

CO 94 (104, 114, 124) sts using smaller needles and long tail cast on or preferred method of cast on. Place marker, and, being careful not to twist, join to work in the round.

Work in seeded rib for 1.25 (1.5, 1.5, 2) inches / 3 (4, 4, 5) cm.

Change to larger needles.

Work Rnds 1–6 of Roman Stitch chart or words, repeating 2-st pattern 47 (52, 57, 62) times around.

Repeat Rnds 1–6 until piece measures 7 (7.25, 7.5, 8) inches / 18 (18.5, 19, 20.5) cm or 1.5 (1.75, 2, 2) inches / 4 (4.5, 5, 5) cm less than desired length.

Begin crown decreases as follows, switching to dpns as needed.

Next Rnd for first size only: [K22, k2tog, k21, k2tog] twice. 90 sts.

Next Rnd for second size only: [K50, k2tog] twice. 102 sts.

Next Rnd for largest size only: [K29, k2tog] four times. 120 sts.

Decrease Set-up Rnd: [K13 (15, 17, 18) sts, k2tog, pm], six times. 84 (96, 108, 114) sts.

Dec Rnd: [Knit to last 2 sts before m, k2tog, sm] 6 times.

Rep last dec rnd until 6 sts rem.

Finishing

Cut a 6 inches / 15 cm tail to thread through rem live sts. Pull tight and secure.

Using a tapestry needle, weave in all ends.

Steam or wet block to measurements.

Mitt Sizes

S (M, L); shown in size L

Finished Measurements

Circumference: 6.5 (7.25, 8) inches / 16.5 (18.5, 20.5) cm

Length: 8.5 (8.5, 9) inches / 21.5 (21.5, 23) cm

Materials

Cephalopod Traveller (100% merino; 280 yds / 256m per 114g skein); color: Bog of Eternal Stench; 1 skein

US#5 / 3.75mm dpns, or circular needles configured for small circumference knitting

US#4 / 3.5mm dpns, or circular needles configured for small circumference knitting

or needle sizes needed to obtain gauge

Stitch holder or waste yarn

Stitch markers

Yarn needle

Gauge

21 sts and 27 rnds = 4 inches / 10cm in stockinette stitch on larger needles

Pattern Notes

These fingerless mittens are worked in the round from the bottom up beginning with smaller needles and a seeded rib stitch cuff. The body of the mitt is worked in repeats of the Roman Stitch pattern on larger needles. The thumb is worked in stockinette stitch Both the top of the mitt and thumb are worked in garter stitch.

Stitches and Techniques

Seeded Rib

Rnd 1: [K1,p1] to end.

Rnd 2: Knit.

Roman Stitch

 Knit

 Purl

Rnds 1–4: Knit.

Rnd 5: *P1, k1; rep to end of rnd.

Rnd 6: *K1, p1; rep to to end of rnd.

Stockinette Stitch

All Rnds: Knit.

Garter Stitch

Rnd 1: Knit.

Rnd 2: Purl.

Abbreviations

M1L - use tip of LH needle to lift strand between sts from front to back; knit loop tbl (increase)

M1R - use tip of LH needle to lift strand between sts from back to front; knit through front loop (increase)

sm - slip marker

Pattern

(both mitts worked the same)

CO 34 (38, 42) sts using smaller needles and long tail cast on or preferred method of cast on.

Place marker and join to work in the round.

Work in Seeded Rib for 2 inches / 5cm.

Change to larger needles.

Work Rnds 1–6 of Roman Stitch chart, or words repeating 2-st pattern 17 (19, 21) times.

Continue to repeat chart, or words, while working thumb gusset.

Thumb Gusset

Rnd 1: K1, pm, M1L, k1, M1R, pm, work chart or words.

Rnds 2–3: K1, sm, k3, sm, work chart or words.

Rnd 4: K1, sm, M1L, knit to m, M1R, sm, work chart or words.

Rnds 5–6: K1, sm, knit to m, sm, work chart or words.

Rep last 4 rnds until there are 13 (15, 17) sts between markers.

Next Rnd: K1, sm, purl to m, sm, work chart or words.

Next Rnd: K1, sm, bind off sts between markers knitwise, rm, work chart or words.

Top of Mitt

Next Rnd: K1, cast on 1 st, work chart, or words.

Continue in established pattern for 2 inches / 5cm or until desired length.

Purl 1 rnd.

Bind off knitwise.

Finishing

Weave in ends securely. Steam or wet block to measurements.

Forsythe

This is what happens when you're stuck for a pattern name and you live with a Comic Book Guy who happens to be watching Riverdale a lot these days. The chevrons remind me of a much more sophisticated Jughead hat, and in the original Archie comic books Jughead's real name is Forsythe Pendleton "Jughead" Jones III.

Size
M (L, XL)

Finished Measurements
Circumference: 18.5 (20.75, 23) inches / 47 (52.75, 58.5) cm

To fit 18–20 (21–22, 23–24) inch / 45.75–50.75 (53.5–55.75, 58.5–61) cm head

Intended to be worn with no ease

Materials
Madelinetosh Tosh Vintage Worsted (100% Merino; 200 yds / 182 m per 50g skein); color: #358 Dubrovnik, 1 skein

US#6 / 4mm needles, configured for small circumference knitting in the round

1 stitch marker

Yarn needle

Gauge
28 sts and 30 rounds = 4 inches / 10cm in pattern stitch

Pattern
Cast on 128 (144, 160 sts), distribute evenly across your needles, preferably in groups of 16.

Work repeats of Brim chart for 2 (2.5, 3) inches / 5 (6.25, 7.75) cm.

Work main chart once.

Work repeats of brim chart again until hat measures your desired length.

Work crown chart.

Break yarn, leaving a 12 inch / 30.5 cm tail. Thread tail through remaining sts, pull taut.

Finishing
Weave in all ends and block to measurements.

Key

☐ No stitch

⦁ Purl

K1tbl

Ssk

Sl1, k2tog, psso

 1/1/1 LpC

1/1/1 RpC

Crown

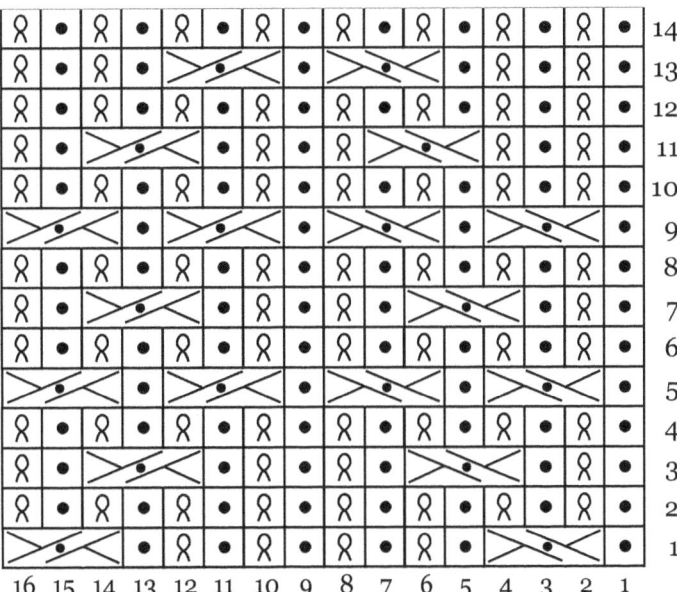

Main

Brim

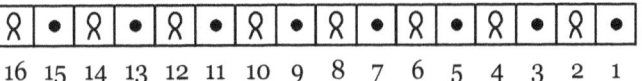

Koray

Koray means "ember moon" in Turkish and there's something about this stitch pattern that reminds me of tilework, so there you go. The A Verb for Keeping Warm yarn is squishy and has that beautiful soft mulespun texture like some of my other favorite yarns (Beaverslide, Shelter). The wool for Pioneer yarn is grown and produced in California. Read more about it on AVFKW's website, it's fascinating!

Size
S (M, L); shown in size M

Finished Measurements
15 (16, 17) inches / circumference at ribbed band before blocking and 16 (17, 18) inches / 40.5 (43, 45.5) cm after

Approximately 9 inches (23 cm) high before and 10 inches (25.5 cm) after (size medium)

Materials
A Verb For Keeping Warm Pioneer Worsted (100% Merino; 160 yds per 50g skein); color: Wolf Lichen; 1 (2, 2) skein(s)

US#5 / 3.75mm needles configured for circular knitting

Stitch markers

Yarn needle

Gauge
20 sts and 28 rounds = 4 inches / 10 cm in pattern stitch

Pattern Notes
This hat really does use up almost all the yarn in the skein if you're doing one of the larger sizes. Be prepared to play yarn chicken!

Stitches and Techniques

Koray stitch pattern (worked over 10 sts)

Rnd 1: P1, k4, k2tog, k3, yo.

Rnds 2, 4, 6 & 8: P5, k5.

Rnd 3: P1, k4, k2tog, k2, yo, k1.

Rnd 5: P1, k4, k2tog, k1, yo, k2.

Rnd 7: P1, k4, k2tog, yo, k3.

Rnd 9: P1, yo, k3, ssk, k4.

Rnds 10, 12, 14 & 16: P1, k5, p4.

Rnd 11: P1, k1, yo, k2, ssk, k4.

Rnd 13: P1, k2, yo, k1, ssk, k4.

Rnd 15: P1, k3, yo, ssk, k4.

Pattern

Using German Twisted, or your favorite stretchy method, cast on 100 (110, 120) sts. Being careful not to twist, join to work in the round, placing a stitch marker to denote the beginning of the round.

Work p1, k1 rib for 3 inches.

Working from either the chart or the pattern words, work 10 (11, 12) repeats of the stitch pattern across the round.

Work Rnds 1–16 2 (3, 3) times.

Work Rnds 1–8 1 (0, 1) time.

Crown

Keeping continuity of pattern as established, work decreases as follows:

Rnd 1: [P2tog, work pattern as set over next 8 sts] 10 (11, 12) times. 90 (99, 108) sts.

Rnd 2: Work as established.

Rnd 3: [P2tog, work in pattern as set over next 7 sts] 10 (11, 12) times. 80 (88, 96) sts.

Rnd 4: Work as established.

Continue decreasing one st per pattern repeat by p2tog, at beginning of pattern repeat, until you have 10 (11, 12) sts. remaining.

Next rnd. [K2tog] 5 (5, 6) times, k1 0 (1, 0) times. 5 (6, 6) sts.

Finishing

Break yarn, weave tail through live sts, fasten off securely and block to measurements.

Key

☐ Knit

• Purl

○ YO

╲ K2tog

╱ Ssk

Chart

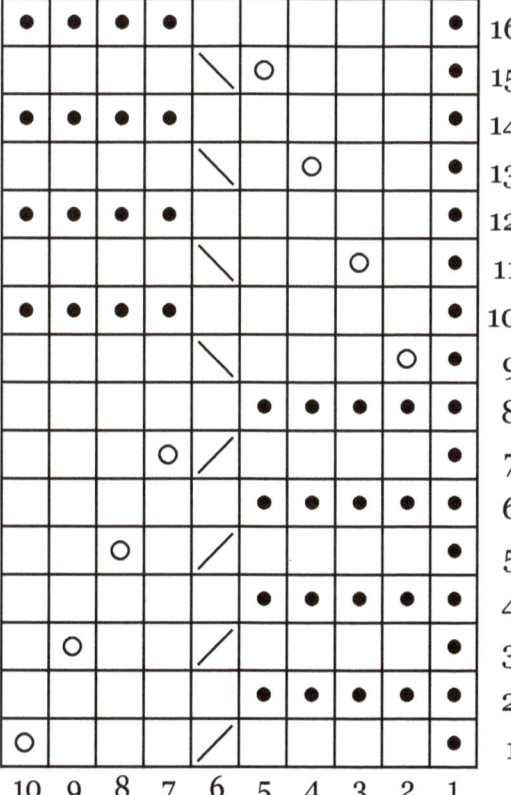

Signy

Signy was the first #knitgrrl52 pattern release. Signy is an old Norse name that means "new victory" and that seems to sum up what we're trying to achieve with this project nicely. A beautifully-textured hat with bobbles, Signy looks good on just about everyone and is a fun, fast knit.

Sizes

S (M, L)

Intended to be worn with 1–2 inches / 2.54–5 cm of negative ease.

Finished Measurements

Crown circumference 20 (22, 24) inches / 50.8 (55.88, 60.96) cm

Materials

Model 1: Clara Yarn Cormo 1.0 Worsted (100% Wool; 155 yds / 142m per 3.32 oz / 94g skein); color: Natural; 1 skein

Model 2: The Plucky Knitter Primo Worsted (75% merino, 20% Cashmere, 5% Nylon; 200 yds per 105g skein); color: Hi Ho Silver; 1 skein

US#8 / 5mm needles, configured for circular knitting (one long circ, two smaller circs, dpns) - or needles required to achieve gauge.

Yarn needle

Gauge

20 sts and 24 rounds = 4 inches / 10cm in pattern stitch

Pattern Notes

Sharply pointed needles are recommended for working the bobbles

Stitches and Techniques

Signy stitch pattern

Rnd 1: [P4, k1] twice

Rnd 2 (and all even rnds): As Rnd 1.

Rnds 3, 5, 7, 9, 11: P4, k1, p4, MB.

Rnd 13: As Rnd 1.

Rnds 15, 17, 19, 21, 23: P4, MB, p4, k1.

Rnd 24: As Rnd 1.

Pattern

Cast on 90 (100, 110) sts, and being careful not to twist, join to work in the round.

Rnd 1: *P1, k1; repeat from * to end of rnd.

Repeat Rnd 1 10 more times.

If working from the chart, follow the chart to Rnd 48.

If working from pattern words, continue as follows:

Rnds 12, 13 & 14: *P4, k1; repeat from * to end of rnd.

Rnds 15, 17, 19, 21 & 23: *P4, k1, p4, MB; repeat from * to end of rnd.

Rnds 16, 18, 20, 22, 24, 25 & 26: *P4, k1; repeat from * to end of rnd.

Rnds 27, 29 & 31: *P4, MB, p4, k1; repeat from * to end of rnd.

Rnd 28 & 30: As Rnd 16.

Work crown decreases as follows:

Rnd 32: *P2tog tbl, p2, k1, p4, k1; repeat from * to end of rnd.

Rnd 33: *P3, MB, p4, k1; repeat from * to end of rnd.

Rnd 34: *P2tog tbl, p1, k1, p4, k1; repeat from * to end of rnd.

Rnd 35: *P2, MB, p4, k1; repeat from * to end of rnd.

Rnd 36: *P2tog tbl, k1, p4, k1; repeat from * to end of rnd.

Rnd 37: *P1, k1, p4, k1; repeat from * to end of rnd.

Rnd 38: *Ssk, p4, k1; repeat from * to end of rnd.

Rnd 39: *K1, p4, k1; repeat from * to end of rnd.

Rnd 40: *P2tog tbl, p3, k1; repeat from * to end of rnd.

Rnd 41: *P4, k1; repeat from * to end of rnd.

Rnd 42: *P2tog tbl, p2, k1; repeat from * to end of rnd.

Rnd 43: *P3, k1; repeat from * to end of rnd.

Rnd 44: *P2tog tbl, p1, k1; repeat from * to end of rnd.

Rnd 45: *P2, k1; repeat from * to end of rnd.

Rnd 46: *P2tog tbl, k1; repeat from * to end of rnd.

Rnd 47: *P1, k1: repeat from * to end of rnd.

Rnd 48: *Ssk; repeat from * to end of rnd.

Rnd 49: Break yarn, leaving a 10 inch tail. Thread yarn through remaining sts, and pull tight.

Finishing

Weave in all ends. Block.

Key

- ▨ No stitch
- ☐ Knit
- • Purl
- ◺ Ssk
- ⊻ P2togtbl
- B MB: Make bobble

Chart

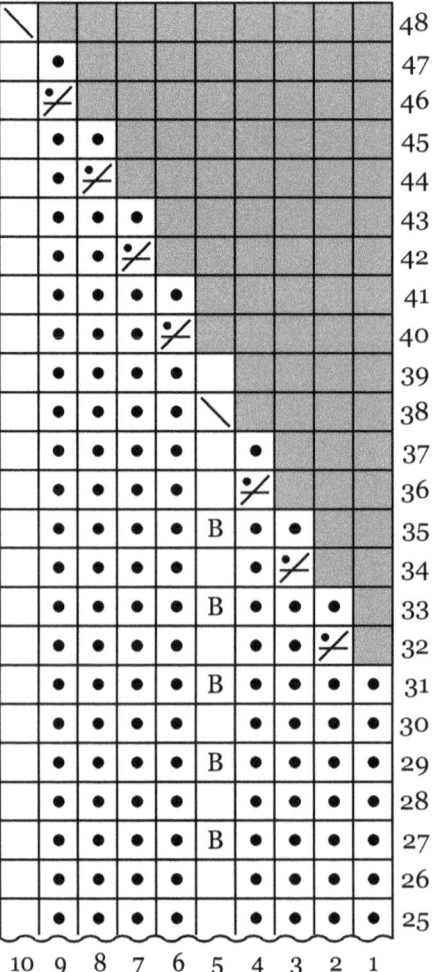

42

Sini

About last night... a few things about this hat are a little bit wonky. The cable stitch pattern is a drunken cable, which means the cables are worked closed together instead of regularly spaced apart. Then the placement of the cable itself is a bit askew. Although the placement of this cable is worked at the beginning of the round (for ease), the hat is worn with the cable off center.

Size

S (M, L, 1X); shown in size M

Finished Measurements

Circumference: 18.5 (20.25, 22, 23.75) inches / 47 (51.5, 56, 60.5) cm

Length: 8 (8.5, 8.5, 9) inches / 20.5 (21.5, 21.5, 23) cm

Materials

Malabrigo Mecha (100% merino; 130 yds / 119m per 100g skein); color: Azul Fresco; 1 skein

US#10 / 6mm 16-inch circular needle, or size needed to obtain gauge

US#10 / 6mm dpns

US#9 / 5.5mm 16-inch circular needle (or dpns) for brim

Stitch marker

Cable needle

Yarn needle

Gauge

14 sts and 22 rnds = 4 inches / 10cm in reverse stockinette stitch on larger needles or size needed to obtain correct gauge

Pattern Notes

This beanie is worked in the round from the bottom up beginning with smaller needles and a single rib stitch brim. The body of the hat is worked in reverse stockinette stitch pattern on larger needles. A drunken cable runs the length of the hat from the bottom of the rim to the top of the crown. The crown is worked in reverse stockinette stitch in swirl decreases. If a slouchy hat style is desired simply add an extra 1-2 inches in length to the crown before beginning the crown decreases.

Stitches and Techniques

Drunken Cable Stitch (multiple of 20 sts)

Rnds 1-4: Knit.

Rnd 5: K10, 5/5 LC.

Rnd 6: Knit.

Rnd 7: 5/5 RC, k10.

Rnds 8-10: Knit.

5/5 LC (left cross): slip 5 sts onto cable needle and hold in front, k5, k5 from cable needle

5/5 RC (right cross): slip 5 sts onto cable needle and hold in back, k5, k5 from cable needle

Pattern

Hatband

Using smaller needles, and long tail method, cast on 65 (71, 77, 83) sts. Being careful not to twist, join to work in the round, placing a marker to denote beginning of rnd.

Set-up round: K20, p1, *k1, p1; repeat from * to end of rnd.

Rnd 1: Work Rnd 1 of cable chart over first 20 sts, p1, *k1, p1; repeat from * to end of rnd.

Continue in established pattern until Rnds 1-10 of cable chart have been worked once.

For S and M sizes: Move onto Body of Hat.

For L and 1X sizes: Continue in pattern for another 3 rnds, then move onto Body of Hat.

Body of Hat

Change to larger needles.

Continue to work cable chart for first 20 sts, purl to end.

Continue in established pattern until hat measures 6 (6.5, 6.5, 7) inches / 15 (16.5, 16.5, 18) cm or 2 inches / 5cm less than desired length.

Crown

Begin crown decreases and switch to dpns when circumference is too small for circulars.

Set-up Rnd: Decrease 5 (1, 7, 3) sts evenly as follows:

Size Small:

K20, [p6, p2tog] five times, p5. 60 sts.

Size Medium:

Work as established until last 2 sts, p2tog. 70 sts.

Size Large:

K20, p1, [p6, p2tog] 7 times. 70 sts.

Size 1x:

K20, p15, [p2tog, p14] three times. 80 sts.

All sizes:

Dec Rnd 1: [K8, k2tog] twice, [p8, p2tog] 4 (5, 5, 6) times. 54 (63, 63, 72) sts.

Dec Rnd 2: [K7, k2tog] twice, [p7, p2tog] 4 (5, 5, 6) times. 48 (56, 56, 64) sts.

Dec Rnd 3: [K6, k2tog] twice, [p6, p2tog] 4 (5, 5, 6) times. 42 (49, 49, 56) sts.

Continue decreasing as established until 6 (7, 7, 8) sts remain.

M (L, 1X) only: K2tog, (p2tog) 2 (2, 3) times, p0 (1, 1, 0) st. 4 (4, 4) sts.

Cut a 6 inch / 15cm tail to thread through remaining live sts. Pull tight and secure.

Finishing

Weave in all ends with yarn needle. Steam or wet block to measurements.

Key

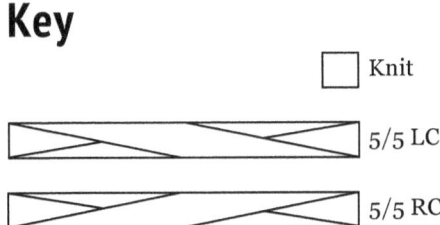

- Knit
- 5/5 LC
- 5/5 RC

Chart

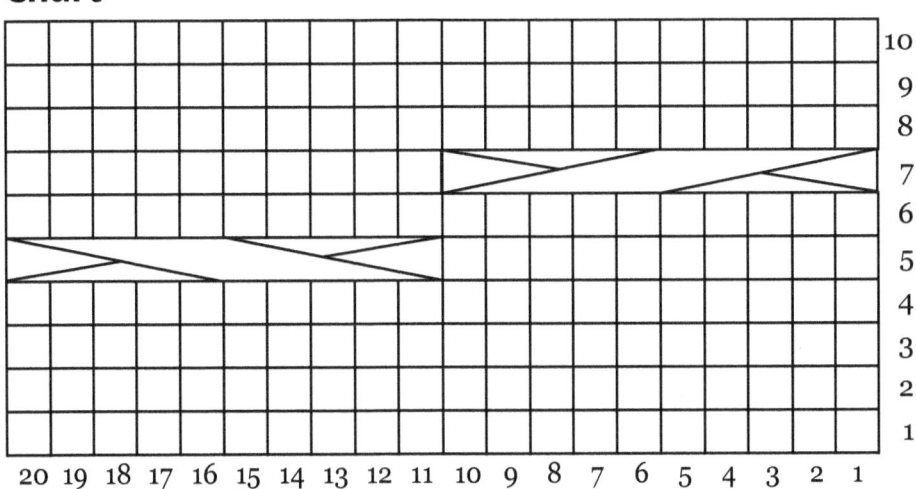

Wickson

Wickson is an unusually sweet type of crab apple that is increasingly being used for hard cider production. Like a good cider, which strives to balance sweet, tart and acidic/tannic variables, the cables in this hat are relatively simple, but when combined in tight succession create a single, beautiful and very dense fabric that makes the most of this beautiful lightweight yarn. Cheers!

Size

S (M, L)

Intended to be worn with 1–2 inches / 2.5–5 cm of negative ease

Finished Measurements

Circumference 20 (22, 24) inches / 50.75 (55.75, 61) cm

Materials

A Verb For Keeping Warm Creating Superwash Sock (100% Merino; 385 yds / 352m per 100g / 3.53 oz skein); color: French Monk's Finest; 1 skein

US#1 / 2.5mm needles configured for circular knitting

US#3 / 3.25mm needles configured for circular knitting

Cable needle

Stitch marker

Yarn needle

Gauge

36 sts and 40 rounds = 4 inches / 10cm in pattern stitch (unblocked and unstretched)

Note: The cable pattern makes a *very* dense fabric that has quite a lot of stretch.

Pattern Notes

If you tend to knit tightly, you may need to go up a needle size to get gauge. If you're not the swatching type and prefer to dive right in, be sure to try the hat on a few inches in to make sure it's stretching enough for your head size!

Stitches and Techniques

Chart A

Rnd 1: 3/2 RC, p1, 3/2 LC, p1.

Rnds 2–4: [K5, p1] twice.

Chart B

Rnd 1: 3/2 RC, p1, 3/2 LC, p1.

Rnds 2–3: [K5, p1] twice.

Rnd 4: K2tog, k3, p1, k3, ssk, p1.

Rnd 5: 2/2 RC, p1, 2/2 LC, p1.

Rnds 6–7: [K4, p1] twice.

Rnd 8: K2tog, k2, p1, k2, ssk, p1.

Rnd 9: 2/1 RC, p1, 2/1 LC, p1.

Rnd 10: [K3, p1] twice.

Rnd 11: K2tog, k1, p1, k1, ssk, p1.

Rnd 12: [k2, p1] twice.

Rnd 13: 1/1 RC, p1, 1/1 LC, p1.

Rnd 14: [K2, p1] twice.

Rnd 15: Ssk, p1, k2tog, p1.

Rnd 66: [K1, p1] twice.

Rnd 17: Sl1, k2tog, psso, p1.

Rnd 18: K1, p1.

Pattern

Using US#1 / 2.5mm needles, and German Twisted, or your favorite stretchy method, cast on 180 (192, 204) sts. Being careful not to twist, join to work in the round, placing a marker to denote the beginning of the round.

Rnd 1: *K2, p1; repeat from * to end of rnd.

Work repeats of Rnd 1, until rib measures 2 inches / 5cm.

Switch to US#3 / 3.25mm needles, and work repeats of Chart A until hat measures 6 (6.5, 7) inches / 15.25 (16.5, 17.75) cm from cast on.

Work Rnds 1–18 of Chart B.

30 (32, 34) sts remain after Rnd 18 of Chart B.

Rnd 19: *Ssk; repeat from * to end of rnd. 15 (16, 17) sts.

Rnd 20:

Size Small:

[Ssk] 7 times, k1. 8 sts.

Size Medium:

[Ssk] 8 times. 8 sts.

Size Large:

[Ssk] 8 times, k1. 9 sts.

Break yarn, leaving a long tail. With yarn needle, thread through remaining loops a couple of times, and pull tight.

Finishing

Weave in all ends and block to measurements.

Key

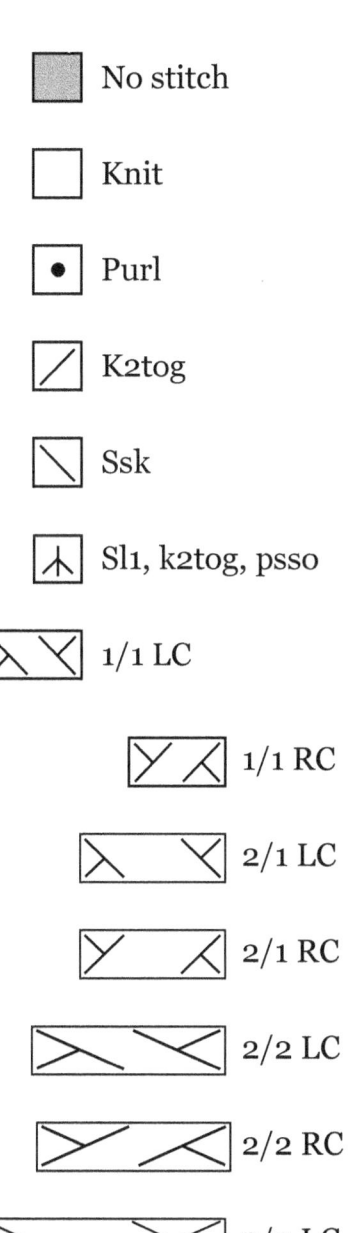

- No stitch
- Knit
- Purl
- K2tog
- Ssk
- Sl1, k2tog, psso
- 1/1 LC
- 1/1 RC
- 2/1 LC
- 2/1 RC
- 2/2 LC
- 2/2 RC
- 3/2 LC
- 3/2 RC

Chart A

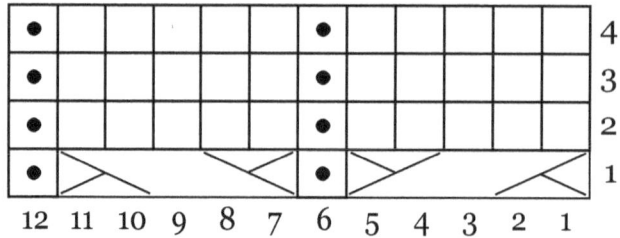

Chart B

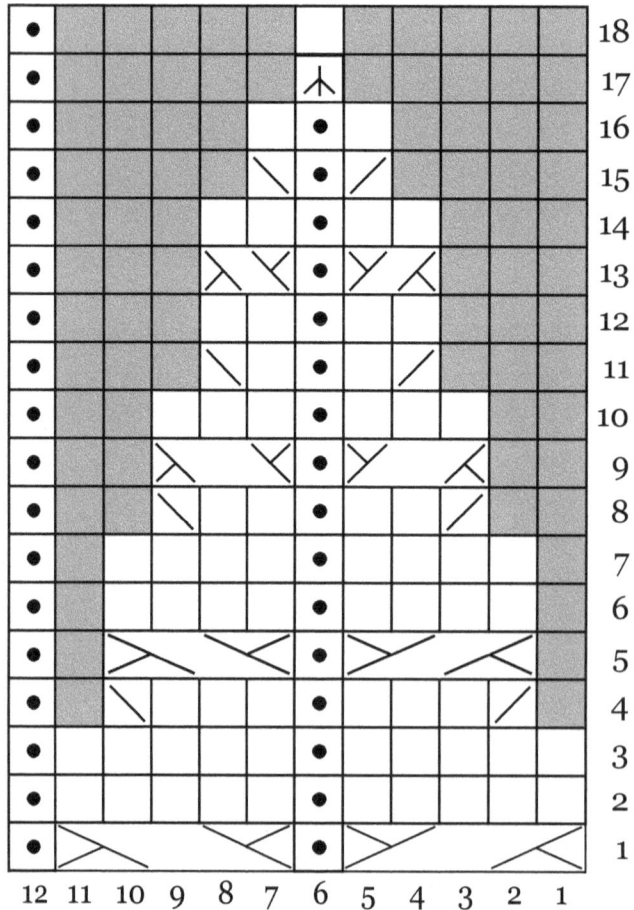

Xantho

This hat is named after **Xanthoparmelia**, *a particularly pretty form of lichen, in homage to the Lichen and Lace yarn used to knit it! I'm not sure if this is one of the many types of lichen that can be used to dye yarn (see photos in my book* **Spin to Knit** *for some of the gorgeous purples you can get from lichen dyes), but it's definitely one you'll see often in the forests near me.*

Size

M (L, 1X, 2X)

Finished Measurements

Crown: 16.75 (19.25, 21.5, 24) inches / 42.5 (49, 54.5, 61) cm

To be worn with one inch of negative ease.

Materials

Lichen and Lace 4ply Worsted (100% Superwash Merino; 200 yds per 115g skein; color: Soot; 1 skein

US#8 / 5mm circular needle, or needle needed to achieve gauge

1 stitch marker

Cable needle

Yarn needle

Gauge

20 sts and 26 rounds = 4 inches / 10cm in stockinette st

Stitches and Techniques

Xantho stitch pattern:

Rnds 1, 2, 4, 5, 6, 8: [P1, k5] twice.

Rnd 3: P1, 3/2 LC, p1, k5.

Rnd 7: P1, k5, p1, 3/2 LC.

Pattern

Cast on 84 (96, 108, 120) sts. Being careful not to twist, join to work in the round, placing a marker at the join to denote the beginning of the round.

Rnd 1: *P1, k2; repeat to end of rnd.

Repeat Rnd 1 until rib measures 3 (3.5, 4, 4) inches / 7.5 (9, 10, 10) cm.

Work Rnds 1–8 of the Xantho chart or stitch pattern words a total of 8 times or until your desired length.

Working from either the chart, or the decreases below, work the crown decreases.

Crown decreases

Rnd 9: *P1, k5, p1, k3, k2tog; repeat from * around.

Rnd 10 (and all even rnds): Work sts as they appear.

Rnd 11: *P1, 3/2 LC, p1, k2, k2tog; repeat from * around.

Rnd 13: *P1, k5, p1, k1, k2tog; repeat from * around.

Rnd 15: *P1, k5, p1, k2tog; repeat from * around.

Rnd 17: *P1, k5, k2tog; repeat from * around.

Rnd 19: *P1, 2/2 LC, k2tog; repeat from * around.

Rnd 21: *P1, k3, k2tog; repeat from * around.

Rnd 23: *P1, k2, k2tog; repeat from * around.

Rnd 25: *P1, k1, k2tog; repeat from * around.

Rnd 27: *P1, k2tog; repeat from * around.

Rnd 29: *K2tog; repeat from * around.

Rnd 30: Break yarn, leaving a 10 inch tail. Thread the tail onto the yarn needle, and draw through the remaining live sts twice.

Finishing

Pull thread tight to close, and weave in ends securely.

Key

No stitch
Knit
Purl
K2tog
Ssk
3/2 LC
2/2 LC

Chart

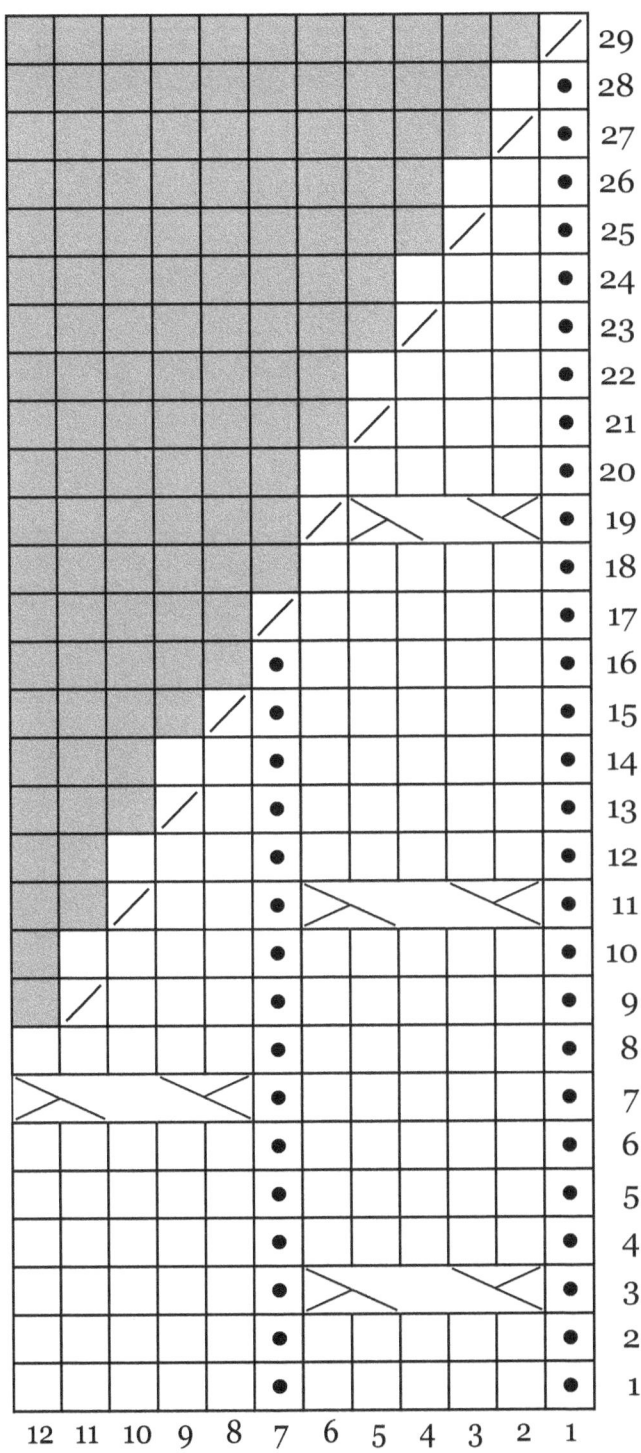

Abbreviations

- **1/1 LC** – place next st on cn, hold in front, k1, k1 from cn
- **1/1 RC** – place next st on cn, hold in back, k1, k1 from cn
- **1/1/1 LpC** – slip 1 st to cn, hold in front, k1tbl, p1, (k1tbl) from cn
- **1/1/1 RpC** – slip 2 sts to cn, hold in back, k1tbl, (p1, k1tbl) from cn
- **2/1 LC** – place next 2 sts on cn, hold in front, k1, k2 from cn
- **2/1 RC** – place next st on cn, hold in back, k2, k1 from cn
- **2/2 LC** – place next 2 sts on cn, hold in front, k2, k2 from cn
- **2/2 RC** – place next 2 sts on cn, hold in back, k2, k2 from cn
- **3/2 LC** – place next 3 sts on cn, hold in front, k2, k3 from cn
- **3/2 LC** – slip 3 sts to cable needle, k2, k3 from cable needle
- **3/2 RC** – place next 2 sts on cn, hold in back, k3, k2 from cn
- **5/5 LC** (left cross): slip 5 sts onto cable needle and hold in front, k5, k5 from cable needle
- **5/5 RC** (right cross): slip 5 sts onto cable needle and hold in back, k5, k5 from cable needle
- **cn** – cable needle
- **k** – knit
- **k1tbl** – knit through back loop
- **k2tog** – knit 2 sts together
- **kfb** – knit into front and back of next st
- **M1L** – use tip of LH needle to lift strand between sts from front to back; knit loop tbl (increase)
- **M1R** – use tip of LH needle to lift strand between sts from back to front; knit through front loop (increase)
- **MB** – make bobble: (k1, p1, k1, p1, k1) into next st, turn, k5, turn, slip 2 sts, k3tog, pass 2 slipped sts over
- **p** – purl

- **p2togtbl** – purl 2 sts together through the back loop
- **pm** – place marker
- **rnd(s)** – round(s)
- **RS** – right side
- **sl1, k2tog, psso** – slip 1 st, k2tog, pass slipped st over – 2 sts decreased
- **sm** – slip marker
- **ssk** – slip as to knit, slip as to purl, knit the 2 slipped sts together
- **st(s)** – stitch(es)
- **W&T** – wrap and turn
- **Wrap 3 st** – [with yarn in back, slip next 3 sts to RH needle, bring yarn to front, slip 3 sts back to LH needle] 3 times, k1tbl, p1, k1tbl.
- **WS** – wrong side
- **yo** – yarn over

Patron thanks

Almost 300 patrons signed on to support #knitgrrl52 on Patreon from its launch and through the first year. Without their financial support and enthusiasm for the project, I could not possibly have taken on something of this size and complexity. I am incredibly grateful for all of my supporters! This list is current as of 15 May 2018—I plan to continue the Patreon in a modified format, so check out patreon.com/knitgrrl to find out what's going on now! Again, my deepest thanks to all of you!

A. Robin Avila
Afton Koontz
Alicia Harder
Aliza Nevarie
Allison King
Amber F. Lee
Amy Duvendack / BadAmy Knits
Amy Lipkowitz
Amy O'Malley
Amy Shelton
Anna Correll
Anne Smith
Annette Wilhelm
Annie Vanaskie Watters
Antje Gillingham
April Ridgeway
Billy Zayac
Bonnie Callahan
Bonnie Groening
Caitlin Bright

Candice Bailey
Cara Henderson
Carole Chesser
Carolina
Carolyn Blakelock
Carolyn Myers
Catherine Dean
CathiBeaStevenson
Ceri Davies
Charles KNITexan
Chelsea Loo
Cheryl Monroe
Cherylann Schmidt
Chloe Sparkle
Chris Lynch
Christine Jones
Christine Tubbs
Christine Widgren
Conchi Rodes
Crystal Hanson

Dana Kashubeck
Danielle Taylor
Deborah Jackson Weiss
Debra Husby
Debrielle Welch
Dee Minturn
Deenna Dains
Deirdre McNeill
Denise Pratt
Diane Nishri
Dianne Shantz
Dindy Yokel
Donna Hulka
Dorce Campbell
Dragonfly Fibers
Duranee Dodson
Eileen Gruber
Eliza Sheppard
Elizabeth Green
Elizabeth Stromme

Elizabeth Theresa
Ellen Boucher
Erin Mullins
Erin Wolff
Esther Bozak
Faith Love
firstfallen
Fran Bee
Frances McCarthy
Gail E. Maddox
Gaye Houchin-Copeland
Gayle Clow
Glenna Eastwood
Glori Medina
Hanna Hintikka
Hazel Daguiar
Heather Ordover
Heather Risher
Irene Speir
Ivete Tecedor
Jacquilynne Schlesier
Jamie Wang
Jan Arnow
Jan Campagne
Janet Clark
Janice Stenger
Janine Le Cras
Jean Belman-Herrera
Jean Link
Jeanne Tufano
Jeff Pinto
Jenn Ridley
Jenn Wisbeck
Jennifer DeAlmeida

Jennifer Hovis
Jennifer Lindberg
Jennifer Wollesen
Jenny Dicastri
Jenny Schoohs
Jerre Dawson
Jessica Steele
Jessica Stowell
Jillana Holt-Reuter
Joan Grahlfs
Johanna Bowline
Julia Johnson-Roy
Julia Kerbl
Julia Knitterlythings
Julie Aronson
Julie Lindsey
Karen Boykin
Karen Fazioli
Kate Brehe
Kate Graham
Kathryn Beyers
Kathy Beaumont
Katie Hughes
Kelsey Leib
Keri McIntyre
Kim Burkhardt
Kim Fuller
Kimberlee Gillis-Bridges
Kitty Hamersma
Knitty Magazine / Amy Singer
Kristin Hansen
LA Bourgeois
Laura Gilman

Laura, Ben & the 4 Dog Crew
Laurel Luchsinger
Laurie Johnson
Laurie Starr
Lea Vollmer
Lee Bernstein
Leni McCormick
Lesley Robinson
Leslie Behm
Linda Hawkins
Linda Randall
Linda Schiffer
Linda Sutherland
Linda Walker
Lise McKinney
Liz Gipson
Lora Felts
Lorraine Dolsen
Louisa
Lynn
Lynne Wolters
Magda Stryk Therrien
Margie Smith
Marie Amer-Westmeyer
Marie Bryan
Marie Duquette
Marion Gibson
Marion Regeste
Marsha Auguste
Marta Poling
Mary Dagnan Wills
Maureen Foulds
Meg Helmes

Melissa Gaul	Psuke Bariah	Sue Roth
Melissa Hellman	Rachel Clark	Susan Burgerman
Melissa Taylor	Ray Janikowski	Susan Jones
Merlene	Raymonda Schwartz	Susan Miller
Merry Rubins	Rebecca Armstrong	Susan Wilson
Merryl Rosenthal	Relaxing With Yarn	Sylvia McFadden
Meryl Dorey	Robin Stewart	Sytske Corver
Michelle Heckman	Rosemary Moore	Tammy Moorse
Michelle K	Sabrina Pauch	Tan A Summers
Michelle Kennedy	Sam B.	Teresa Dannemiller
Michelle Toich	Sandra Fleming	Teresa Emery
Monika Stramaglia	Sandra Zetterlund	Terri
Nan	Sandy Kolher	Terri Emery
Natalia Forrest	Sara Beckwith	Terri J. Rau
Natalia Uribe Wilson	Sarah Devantier	Tuulia Salmela
Niki Curtis	Shannon Coon	Ulla Martin
Nyriis	Shelley Harper	Under MeOxter
Pam Daley	Shelley Kinder	Vicki Lynch
Pamela Schultz	Shelly Minton	Virginia R Jones
PariserLandluft	Stacey Melquist	Yael Weiss
Pat Fisher	Stacy Person	ZhanTao Yang
Paula Wilson	Stephanie Mcguckin	

About CP

Cooperative Press was founded in 2007 by Shannon Okey, the author of this book and many others. She had been doing freelance acquisitions work, introducing authors with projects she believed in to editors at various publishers. And although working with traditional publishers can be very rewarding, there are some books that fly under their radar. They're too avant–garde, or the marketing department doesn't know how to sell them, or they don't think they'll sell 50,000 copies in a year.

5,000 or 50,000. Does the book matter to that 5,000? Then it should be published.

In 2009, Cooperative Press (cooperativepress. com) changed its name to reflect the relationships we have developed with authors working on books. We work together to put out the best quality books we can and share in the proceeds accordingly.

Thank you for supporting independent publishers and authors.

Cooperative Press can be found on

- Facebook: http://www.facebook.com/cooperativepress
- Instagram: http://www.instagram.com/cooperativepress
- Ravelry: http://www.ravelry.com/people/cooperativepress
- Web/shop: http://cooperativepress.com

  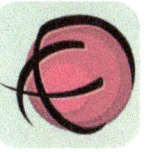

www.ingramcontent.com/pod-product-compliance
Lightning Source LLC
Chambersburg PA
CBHW042135160426
43199CB00022B/2918